Country ABCs

Israel ABCs

A Book About the People and Places of Israel

Written by Holly Schroeder • Illustrated by Claudia Wolf

Special thanks to our advisers for their expertise:
Esther Raizen, Ph.D.
Associate Professor of Middle Eastern Studies
The University of Texas at Austin

Susan Kesselring, M.A., Literacy Educator
Rosemount-Apple Valley-Eagan (Minnesota) School District

PICTURE WINDOW BOOKS
Minneapolis, Minnesota

Managing Editor: Bob Temple
Creative Director: Terri Foley
Editor: Nadia Higgins
Editorial Adviser: Andrea Cascardi
Copy Editor: Laurie Kahn
Designer: John Moldstad
Page production: Picture Window Books
The illustrations in this book were prepared digitally.

Picture Window Books
5115 Excelsior Boulevard
Suite 232
Minneapolis, MN 55416
1-877-845-8392
www.picturewindowbooks.com

Copyright © 2004 by Picture Window Books
All rights reserved. No part of this book may be reproduced without written permission from the publisher. The publisher takes no responsibility for the use of any of the materials or methods described in this book, nor for the products thereof.

Printed in the United States of America.

Library of Congress Cataloging-in-Publication Data
Schroeder, Holly.
Israel ABCs : a book about the people and places of Israel / written by Holly Schroeder ; illustrated by Claudia Wolf.
p. cm. — (Country ABCs)
Summary: Each letter of the alphabet is represented by illustrations and information related to Israel.
Includes bibliographical references and index.
ISBN 1-4048-0179-0 (hardcover)
ISBN 1-4048-0357-2 (softcover)
1. Israel—Juvenile literature. [1. Israel. 2. Alphabet.]
I. Wolf, Claudia, ill. II. Title. III. Series.
DS118 .S365 2004
956.94—dc22
2003016520

Shalom! (sha-LOME)

"Peace." This is how Israelis greet one another in Hebrew.

Marhaba! (MAR-ha-ba)

And this is how they say "hello" in Arabic, Israel's second official language.

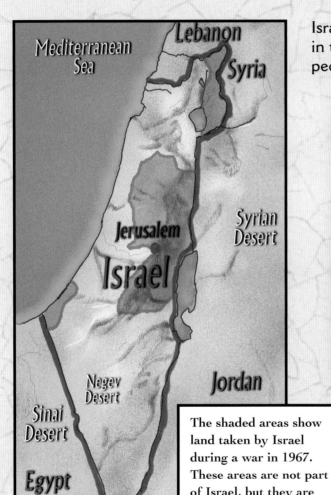

Israel is a small country in the Middle East. It is the only country in the world in which most people are Jewish. About six million people live in Israel. It ranks 100th in world population.

The shaded areas show land taken by Israel during a war in 1967. These areas are not part of Israel, but they are controlled by the Israeli government.

Hebrew and Arabic don't use the same letters that we use to write English.

This is how you write *shalom* in Hebrew: שלום

This is how you write *marhaba* in Arabic: مرحبا

A is for Abraham.

Aa

Abraham was a Jewish leader. The story of his life is told in the Bible. After a time, most of the Jews were driven out of the land and scattered around the world. Since then, many other peoples have lived in the area. Jews started coming back to the land in large numbers about 120 years ago. The county that we know today as Israel began in 1948.

FAST FACT: Arabs are the second largest group of people in Israel. They believe Abraham's son Ishmael was the first ancestor of their people.

Bb

B is for Bedouin.

Bedouins are Arab people who come from Israel's deserts. Some Bedouins still live much the way their ancestors did 1,500 years ago. They live in tents. They travel from place to place looking for food and water for their camels, goats, and sheep.

FAST FACT: Today, many Bedouins live in towns. Some Bedouins work as tour guides on desert safaris.

C is for cactus fruit.

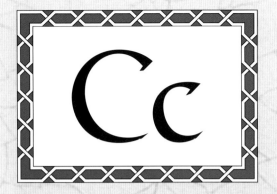

Israeli street vendors sell cactus fruit to hungry passersby. A cactus fruit is called *tsabar* in Hebrew. *Tsabar* is also a nickname for a person who was born in Israel. People joke that a native Israeli is prickly on the outside but sweet inside, just like cactus fruit.

D is for Dead Sea.

The Dead Sea isn't really a sea. It is a very salty lake—about nine times saltier than the ocean. It's called the Dead Sea because no plants or fish can live in it. The water is so thick with salt that a person can float on top of it and read a magazine.

FAST FACT: *The trip to the Dead Sea is so steep that people's ears pop as they're driving. The Dead Sea is the lowest place on earth, at 1,339 feet (408 meters) below sea level.*

7

E is for Elat.

Ee

Schools of colorful fish swim in the waters off the coast of Elat, a city on the very southern tip of Israel. People come from all around the world to snorkel by its famous coral reef. They wear special masks that let them breathe underwater. They spend hours watching beautiful creatures glide by.

FAST FACT: Elat is Israel's port to the Gulf of Aqaba, which leads to the Red Sea. The port is very helpful because it gives Israel's ships a shortcut to Asia and Australia.

F is for flag.

The Israeli flag features the six-pointed Star of David. The star is made up of two triangles on top of each other. (One triangle is right-side up, and the other is upside down.) There is a saying that just as the triangles cannot be broken apart, neither can the Israeli people. Above and below the star are blue stripes. These look like the stripes on a Jewish prayer shawl.

G is for gold dome.

Gg

A gold dome shimmers in the skyline of Jerusalem, Israel's most famous city. The dome is coated with 176 pounds (80 kilograms) of real gold. It caps an ancient building called the Dome of the Rock. Muslims from all around the world go there to pray. They believe it marks the place where their leader, the prophet Muhammad, went up to heaven.

H is for Hebrew.

One hundred years ago, very few people spoke Hebrew. Hebrew had been the language Jews used in prayer. It hadn't been used in daily life for almost 2,000 years. With the creation of Israel, the Jewish people decided they needed one language they could all understand. They learned to speak their original language.

FAST FACT: Hebrew has 22 letters, which are read from right to left.

11

I is for ibex.

Part of the fun of hiking in Israel's deserts is trying to spot an ibex. Hikers listen for the high whistling sound of this rare wild goat. They look for the male ibex's long, curved horns.

FAST FACT: *Most of Israel's ibex live on nature reserves. A nature reserve is a protected area of land where wildlife can live in peace.*

J is for Jerusalem.

Jj

During the time of the Bible, Jerusalem was an important religious center. Today, the city is still rich with stories and landmarks from its long past. Jerusalem is a holy city for Jews, Christians, and Muslims. Together, these groups make up more than one-half of all the people in the world.

This is a scene from Jerusalem's Old City. Most of the winding stone streets in this part of the city are too narrow for cars.

K is for Knesset.

The Knesset is Israel's ruling body of government. It is made up of 120 members. Israel has a president, but its most powerful leader is the prime minister.

The Knesset building

L is for lunar calendar.

A lunar calendar doesn't begin in January and end in December. It has its own months, which are based on the phases of the moon. Jews use a lunar calendar to figure out when their religious holidays are. Rosh Hashanah, the Jewish New Year, is the first day of the first lunar month. It falls in September or early October.

A ram's horn, or shofar, is blown on Rosh Hashanah.

M is for menorah.

The menorah is a seven-branched candlestick. Almost every Jewish home has one. Menorahs are also displayed in public places around Israel. A huge bronze menorah stands near the Knesset in Jerusalem. It honors the state of Israel.

Nn

N is for new Israeli sheqel (NIS).

Israel's unit of money is called the new Israeli sheqel. *Sheqalim* is the word for more than one sheqel. Sheqalim come in coins and bills, ranging in amounts from 1 to 200. One sheqel is made up of 100 agorot, which are like pennies.

FAST FACT: Israeli money has Hebrew, Arabic, and English words on it.

O is for outdoor markets.

Oo

On narrow streets in Jerusalem's Old City, tourists wander through crowded outdoor markets. The markets smell like spices and freshly baked bread. Arab vendors hang colorful scarves from the tops of their small shops. They pile pillows, bowls, and other souvenirs right on top of the stone streets.

FAST FACT: The mild, dry weather in Israel lets people spend a lot of time outside.

P is for Palestinians.

Pp

Palestinian Arabs have been living in the Middle East for about 1,400 years. Today, about four million Palestinians live in Israel and areas under its control. Israelis and Palestinians fight about who should live on this land. Many people are working on the problem of how the Palestinians and Israelis can live together in peace.

This Palestinian boy's checkered scarf is called a kaffiyeh (ka-FEE-yeh). The kaffiyeh is a symbol of the Palestinian people.

Q is for Qumran.

In 1947, a Bedouin boy went into a cave and found some clay jars. Inside were parchment scrolls, which are thin sheets of leather with writing on them. The scrolls had been written by Jewish people more than 2,000 years earlier. These early Jews lived in a place called Qumran. These scrolls, known as the Dead Sea Scrolls, are very famous. They help us discover what life was like during the time of the Bible.

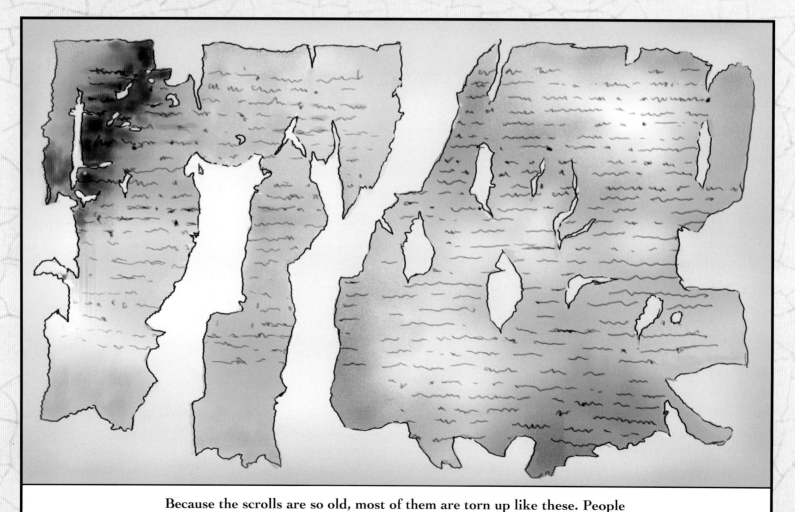

Because the scrolls are so old, most of them are torn up like these. People have spent many years figuring out how to put the scrolls back together.

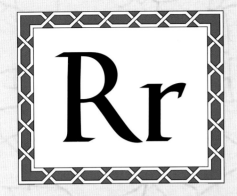

R is for the River Jordan.

In most places, the River Jordan is only about 5 feet (1½ meters) deep. But this shallow, muddy river is one of the most famous rivers in the world. According to the Bible, this is the river where Jesus Christ was baptized. Today, Christians come from around the world to be baptized here as well. They stand in the water while friends and family pray for them.

FAST FACT: Some sections of the River Jordan have fast, rushing water. People like to go rafting on these rough parts of the river.

S is for Sabbath.

Every Friday, starting at sunset, almost all the businesses and restaurants in Israel close down. Friday evening is the beginning of the Jewish Sabbath. The Sabbath, or Shabbat, is a day for resting. It ends after sunset on Saturday. Many Israelis spend the day picnicking or going to soccer games.

FAST FACT: Very religious Jews won't do anything that seems like work on the Sabbath. They won't drive a car or even turn on an oven.

T is for theater.

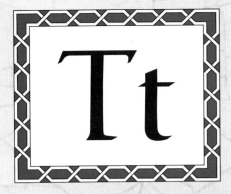

Per person, Israelis go to the theater more than people from any other country. Many shows in Israel are about the fighting between Israelis and the Palestinians. Theater helps Israelis understand the trouble in their country and feel better about it.

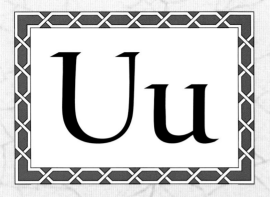

U is for ulpan.

A lot of Israelis are Jews who have come from many different countries. Often, new Israeli citizens don't speak Hebrew. An ulpan is a special school for teaching Hebrew to newcomers. Most ulpans are free for the first six months.

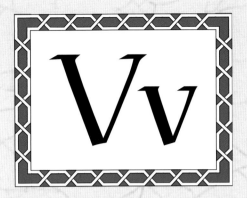

V is for Via Dolorosa.

Via Dolorosa means the Street of Sorrows. It is a famous street in Jerusalem. Christians believe Via Dolorosa is the route Jesus walked on his way to the place where he was put to death. They come from around the world to walk in Jesus' footsteps.

Ww

W is for water.

Farmers in Israel are always careful about using water. Because there are so few sources of water in Israel, farmers try to grow crops that don't need much watering. They rely on a complicated system of canals, pipes, and tunnels to bring water from the north to the south. Much of Israel's dry desert land has been turned into lush, green farms.

FAST FACT: *Sometimes farmers even cover their plants with plastic to keep the plants from drying out.*

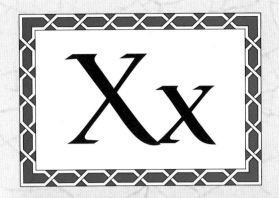

X is for exports.

Oranges, flowers, and computer equipment are some of the main items that Israel exports, or sells, to other countries. Israelis also buy rough diamonds, cut and polish them, and then sell them again. The Israel Diamond Exchange is one of the largest diamond markets in the world.

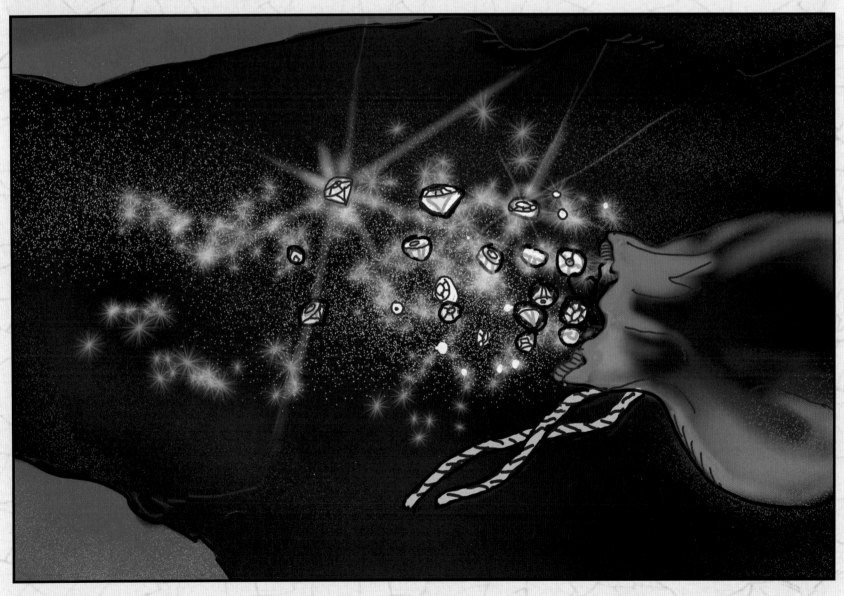

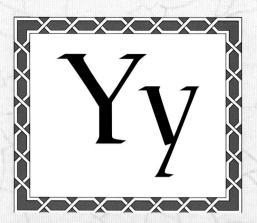

Yy

Y is for yarmulke (YAH-muh-kuh).

A yarmulke is a small round cap worn by some Jewish men and boys. The Hebrew word for yarmulke is *kippah* (kee-PAH). A kippah can be knitted or made of cloth. It comes in many different colors. Covering one's head with a yarmulke is meant as a sign of respect for God and for one's fellow Jews.

FAST FACT: *Israelis can tell something about a man's beliefs by the kind of yarmulke he wears. A black one, for example, shows he is very strict about following religious laws.*

Z is for Zionism.

Zz

Zionism is a movement started in 1897 by Theodor Herzl. His goal was to create a Jewish country. During World War II (1939–45), Jews in Europe needed a place to go to get away from evil treatment by the Nazi government in Germany. Support for the Zionist movement grew, and Israel became a country.

Israel in Brief

Official Name: State of Israel

Capital: Jerusalem

Official languages: Hebrew and Arabic

Population: 6,116,533

Religions: 80% Jewish, 15% Muslim, 5% Christian and other religions

Education: required for children between 6 and 16; free for children up to 18

Major holidays: Passover (March/April); Independence Day (April/May); Shavuot (May/June); Rosh Hashanah (September/October); Yom Kippur (September/October); Hanukkah (November/December)

Transportation: Israel has about one car for every five people. Buses are the main form of public transportation.

Climate: mostly comfortable temperatures; hot and dry in southern and eastern desert areas

Area: 8,019 square miles (20,770 square kilometers)—a little smaller than the state of New Jersey

Highest point: Har Meron, 3,963 feet (1,208 meters)

Lowest point: Dead Sea, 1,339 feet (408 meters) below sea level

Type of government: parliamentary democracy

Head of government: prime minister

Major industries: technology, wood and paper products, cement, diamond cutting

Natural resources: timber, copper ore, natural gas, clay, sand

Major agricultural products: citrus fruits, vegetables, cotton, beef, poultry, dairy products

Chief exports: machinery and equipment, software, cut diamonds, agricultural products

Money: new Israeli sheqel (NIS)

Say It in Israeli Hebrew

hello/good-bye . . . . *sha-LOME*

thank you . . . . *toe-DAH*

please . . . . *be-va-ka-SHA*

How are you? . . . . *ma nish-MA?*

yes . . . . *ken*

no . . . . *loh*

one . . . . *eh-HAD*

two . . . . *SHTA-yim*

three . . . . *sha-LOSH*

Say It in Palestinian Arabic

hello . . . . *MAR-ha-ba*

good-bye . . . . *MA-ahs sa-LAM-ah*

thank you . . . . *SHOOK-run*

How are you? (to a man) . . . . *KEEF-uk?*

How are you? (to a woman) . . . . *KEEF-ik?*

yes . . . . *eh*

no . . . . *laa*

one . . . . *WA-hid*

two . . . . *tin-AIN*

three . . . . *ta-LAA-tay*

Glossary

ancestor—a relative who lived several generations ago

baptize—to pour water on someone as part of a Christian religious practice

Bible—a book written thousands of years ago that is holy to Christians and Jews

Muhammad—the man who started a religion called Islam. Muhammad lived about 1,500 years ago.

Muslim—a follower of a religion called Islam

Star of David—a Jewish symbol that is made up of two triangles on top of each other. One points up, and the other points down. Together, they make a six-pointed star.

To Learn More

At the Library

Gresko, Marcia S. *Israel*. Minneapolis:
    Carolrhoda Books, 2000.

Grossman, Laurie M. *Children of Israel*. Minneapolis:
    Carolrhoda Books, 2000.

Loewen, Nancy. *Food in Israel*. Vero Beach, Fla.:
    Rourke Publications, 1991.

Nye, Naomi Shihab. *The Space Between Our Footsteps:
    Poems and Paintings from the Middle East*.
    New York: Simon & Schuster Books for
    Young Readers, 1998.

Thoennes Keller, Kristin. *Israel*. Mankato, Minn.:
    Bridgestone Books, 1999.

On the Web

Fact Hound

Fact Hound offers a safe, fun way to find Web sites related to this book.
All of the sites on Fact Hound have been researched by our staff.
http://www.facthound.com

1. Visit the Fact Hound home page.
2. Enter a search word related to this book,
    or type in this special code: 1404801790.
3. Click on the FETCH IT button.

Your trusty Fact Hound will fetch the best sites for you!

Index